T0198556

To order additional copies of this book, contact:
Xlibris
844-714-8691
www.Xlibris.com
Orders@Xlibris.com

ISBN: Softcover   978-1-6641-3447-8
         Hardcover   978-1-6641-3449-2
         EBook   978-1-6641-3448-5

Library of Congress Control Number: 2020919681

Print information available on the last page.

Rev. date: 10/14/2020

A
NEW YORK CITY
ADVENTURE

PAUL CALABRESE

CONEY ISLAND

Our adventure begins on the south side of Brooklyn, New York. Nestled between the areas of Sea Gate and Brighton Beach and at the final train stop at Stillwell Avenue, Brooklyn's famous Coney Island has long been the playground of New York City.

Often referred to as the poor man's paradise, the Coney Island amusement park has been a favorite destination for locals and tourists alike for many decades. Along with its rich history, this destination also offers a buffet of attractions, such as dining, shopping, games, rides, and the world-famous Coney Island Boardwalk.

Whether you are visiting the newly renovated New York Aquarium or enjoying a day on the beach with friends and family, Coney Island is a haven in Brooklyn, New York, that offers almost endless possibilities for friends and family alike.

After enjoying a concert at the Ford Amphitheater or a Brooklyn Cyclones baseball game at MCU Stadium, we often stop by Nathan's Famous for Coney Island hotdogs and some drinks.

During the summer seasons, we often head to the Coney Island Boardwalk on Friday evenings to view the free and amazing fireworks show while having a sausage and pepper hero at Ruby's Bar and Grill. Recently, many new rides and attractions have been added to Coney Island, yet it still maintains many historic and irreplaceable attractions and rides from days past.

Coney Island was discovered in 1609 by Dutch explorer Henry Hudson. Sea Lion, the first enclosed amusement park in Coney Island, opened in 1895 followed by others such as Steeplechase, Luna Park, Dream Land, and Astroland.

THE NEW YORK CITY SUBWAY

Our journey continues with a quick walk to the Stillwell Avenue entrance to the New York City transit system, located at the corners of Surf Avenue and Stillwell Avenue.

Managed and operated by the Metropolitan Transit Authority (MTA), the first initial fare for the subway system in New York City was only five cents back in the early 1900s. With 472 stations in current operation, the New York City subway system is the largest in the world. Twenty-four hours a day, 7 days a week, 365 days a year, you can count on the subway system to take you to endless adventures in all five boroughs of New York City.

With over 5 million daily riders and almost 2 billion riders annually, the subway systems of New York City are one of the most convenient ways to travel about the city quickly and conveniently.

Heading to unlimited destinations, this subway system has become the arteries and veins of the big city, bringing tourists, families, friends, and commerce together.

Construction on the New York City subway system started in the 1900s, and the first subway line was officially opened in 1904. Since then, the New York City subway system has expanded and grown over the years, connecting all five boroughs of New York City and beyond.

Many newly built or renovated stations recently offer more up-to-date amenities, such as ramps and air conditioning, and even artwork has been added to the subway systems. It is now a far cry from a few decades ago, when the system was littered in graffiti, garbage, and crime. Since then, many changes have been implemented to improve the safety of its patrons and workers, as well as to improve the rider experience for all who use this wonder of transportation.

GRAND CENTRAL TERMINAL

After a short ride on the New York City Subway System, coming from Coney Island in Brooklyn, New York, we decided to unboard our train at the center of the New York City subway system in Manhattan, New York City, we have arrived at Grand Central Terminal.

Located on Forty-Second Street and Park Avenue, Grand Central Terminal—also known as Grand Central Station—opened up in February of 1913 and, since then, has been a landmark of architectural wonder and the heart of mass transit for all residence and visitors of New York City.

Built on over forty-eight acres of prime real estate, Grand Central Terminal offers forty-four platforms and sixty-seven tracks; and with over 750,000 visitors a day, the Grand Central Terminal is well prepared for visitors and travelers, with retail and dining to accommodate all that find themselves at this marvel of New York City.

Open twenty-four hours all year-round, this architectural wonder offers infinite possibilities for all who explore its vast history and modern upgrades.

Famous for, among other things, the four-faced oval clock located at the center of the main concourse, Grand Central Terminal has been the landscape for endless cinema, photography, and artwork throughout the years.

On the dining concourse, close to the famous Oyster Bar, there is a place called the Whispering Gallery, where you can whisper into one of the archways and the person at the opposite corner can hear everything you say as if you were standing next to them.

It is unclear whether or not this was designed to act this way on purpose during construction or if it was just a fluke that nobody expected and wasn't realized until after construction.

TIMES SQUARE

Now that we have traveled far away from the beaches of Coney Island in Brooklyn and we now have arrived in the heart of the city, a quick walk will bring us to the famous Times Square in Midtown Manhattan, which is located at the intersections of Broadway, Seventh Avenue, and Forty-Second Street. It was also originally known years ago as Longacre Square. Times Square was renamed soon after the *New York Times* made home here (as in Times Square). Attracting tens of millions of visitors every year, this visual paradise has a long history.

Going back to the speakeasy and prohibition days of New York City and before and now the mega attraction it has become for tourists to shop, dine and take in all that Times Square has to offer.

Known internationally as the location of the New Year's Eve ball dropping ceremony, as well as so much more, Times Square is often referred to as the center of the world and the number 1 voted place to spend New Year's Eve.

Times Square hosts about 1 million people on the New Year's Eve celebrations and is viewed around the world. Times Square is the most visited tourist attraction in the world with over 40 million visitors annually.

One major attraction are the bright lights from the LED advertisement displays that blanket the walls of the surrounding buildings. Advertising on these LED displays can cost over 4 million dollars a year, and the lights are so bright that Times Square can actually be seen from space.

The first New Year's Eve celebration at Times Square was in 1903, when the *New York Times* newspaper office celebrated the company's opening with a firework show. This was soon replaced with the now famous New Year's ball dropping ceremony. At first, the ball was lowered from a flagpole and then would drop slowly to land at the exact time of the New Year.

CENTRAL PARK

After the hustle and bustle of Times Square, we have decided to take a quick walk uptown to the oasis of Manhattan Central Park.

With over eight hundred acres of real estate smack in the middle of New York City, this was the first public professionally landscaped park in America.

Central Park has been a place for the public and tourists alike to enjoy and find refuge, peace, and tranquility since it was officially opened in 1859. Other than the obvious attractions of wide-open grassy fields and shady trees to picnic under, Central Park has much more to offer.

The Metropolitan Museum of Art, the Central Park Zoo, and more are just some of the great attractions of this park.

Here, you will also find endless activities, such as ice skating, playgrounds, outdoor concerts, biking, jogging, and other sports. There are beautiful statues, amazing fountains, soothing lakes, and historical bridges to explore as well. It is also the home of the famous Strawberry Fields and the Belvedere Castle.

Since the early 1900s, Central Park has been the most filmed public park in the world and has been used in over 240 feature films.

If and when you tire from walking this vast park, you will be glad to know that there are over nine thousand benches scattered throughout the park so visitors and locals can take a break, relax, and enjoy the scenery.

The legendary Central Park has long been an oasis in the middle of the concrete jungle we call Manhattan that surrounds it and is open for all to come and enjoy.

CITY HALL

After a relaxing break in Central Park, we continue our journey with a trip to City Hall, and now that we have arrived at the spectacular City Hall located in City Hall Park, we are in the presence of more than just a place for people to get married.

City Hall is so much more.

This structure is built of brick, marble, and granite. It uses no steel or iron and is the tallest masonry building in the world. More than 88 million bricks were used during its construction, and near the base of the tower, the walls can be up to twenty-two feet thick.

With its incredible architecture and rich history, City Hall is a historical landmark. Built between the years 1803 and 1812, City Hall houses such artifacts as an incredible portrait collection from the nineteenth century consisting of many of the most elite dignitaries of its era. Within the walls of this building holds the offices of the mayor of New York City, the New York City Council and other governmental agencies. You can also find George Washington's desk located in the governor's room.

Located in the Civic Center of Lower Manhattan, City Hall is surrounded by other office buildings as well as high-end residential units, and it is a few short blocks from the Freedom Tower and Wall Street.

City Hall was originally designed by two architects after a fierce competition to win the award. One architect was French, and the other was a local New Yorker. The award was $350.

WALL STREET

Another quick walk and we have arrived at another famous location known to all as the financial hub of the world. Not far from City Hall, on a few blocks of some of the most expensive real estate in the world, is Wall Street.

In the eighteen century, under a buttonwood tree, traders and spectators would gather to trade securities; and in 1792, the traders would form the Buttonwood Agreement, which in turn would soon become the origin of the New York Stock Exchange.

Located on a few square blocks around Wall Street, companies and the government agencies run some of the biggest and most important financial organizations in the world. The US Federal Reserve, the *Wall Street Journal*, the NASDAQ, the New York Mercantile Exchange, and many other banks and financial institutions all operate in this area.

In 1789, George Washington was inaugurated as the first president of the United States at Federal Hall, where now stands his statue. Other attractions include the *Charging Bull* and the Trinity Church. Also close by is the South Street Seaport and the 9/11 Memorial Museum, which is near Battery Park, where you can also take a ferry to the Statue of Liberty.

SOUTH STREET SEAPORT

A quick stroll from Wall Street brings us to the timeless and legendary South Street Seaport.

In 1625, the Dutch West India Company founded the first outpost and pier here, which quickly developed into a hustling seaport.

Due to the location, this area was perfect for ships to load and unload goods from around the world and in calm waters. Nestled in between the Brooklyn and Manhattan shorelines, the waves were often calmer than other areas around the city, making it the most convenient location to receive and deliver goods domestically and internationally.

Located under the Brooklyn Bridge on the Manhattan shoreline, the South Street Seaport is a reminder of days past. With some of the oldest buildings and architecture in New York City, South Street Seaport was the first twenty-four-hour district, which gave birth to the phrase "the city that never sleeps."

Before they traded stocks and bonds in Lower Manhattan on Wall Street, the commerce being traded was tangible goods. These were shipped, bought, sold, and traded from these ports. South Street Seaport was the gateway of international shipping and trading in America and a key factor in the development of the New York City.

The maritime buildings surrounding this port have a rich history of the beginning days of New York City. Although it is now a bustling tourist attraction, South Street Seaport offers a rare glimpse into the past of New York City, with other activities such as dining, shopping, tours, and museums, to name a few. South Street Seaport was once known as the Street of Ships.

ROCKEFELLER CENTER

In 1928, after the great stock market crash, John D. Rockefeller, using a considerable amount of his fortune, leased twenty-two acres from Columbia University. Three years later, in 1931, construction commenced on Rockefeller Center. It was completed in 1939.

This huge location now consists of nineteen high-rise buildings. You can find on top of the Comcast building, on its observation deck, beautiful views of Manhattan and beyond.

In the early 1930s, while Rockefeller Center was being constructed, the construction workers would pool their money together to erect a twenty-foot Christmas tree at this location. This would soon become a tradition that would last to this day and attract millions of visitors over the years during the holiday season.

The lighting of the Christmas tree at Rockefeller Center is an experience enjoyed by millions of people worldwide and also a tradition that has made Rockefeller Center one of the most visited places on earth during the holiday season.

A city within a city, Rockefeller Center is also famous for its world-known skating ring. Gazed upon by the bronze statue of Prometheus, it has long been a favorite destination for families and tourist alike.

THE BRONX ZOO

Now for our final adventure, we've decided to visit the Bronx Zoo in Bronx, New York. Built about the same time as the New York subway system we used to arrive here, the Bronx Zoo opened to the public on November 8, 1899.

Fordham University once owned the property until it was sold for one dollar with the agreement that it would be used as a zoo or garden location. Located at Fordham Road and Bronx River Parkway, the Bronx Zoo is the largest metropolitan zoo in the United States. It is the headquarters for the Wildlife Conservation Society; and with over 265 acres of parkland containing four zoos, over 5,000 animals with 650 different species, and more than 750 full-time employees, the Bronx Zoo attracts more than 2 million visitors a year.

Shopping, tours, shows, food and drink, as well as other endless possibilities await all those who visit this massive zoo with all it has to offer.

The Bronx Zoo is a must-see destination when visiting New York City. It is by far the best and biggest zoo in the five boroughs and offers wonderful possibilities for tourists and local residence alike.

Printed in the United States
By Bookmasters